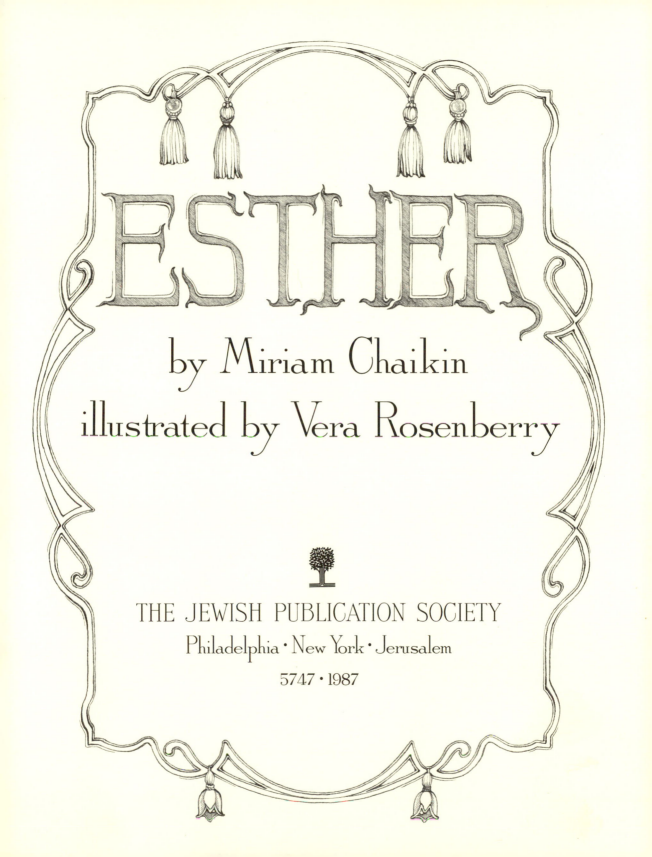

ESTHER

by Miriam Chaikin

illustrated by Vera Rosenberry

THE JEWISH PUBLICATION SOCIETY

Philadelphia · New York · Jerusalem

5747 · 1987

Text copyright © 1987 by The Jewish Publication Society
Illustrations copyright © 1987 by Vera Rosenberry
First edition   All rights reserved
Manufactured in the United States of America
Library of Congress Cataloging in Publication Data

Chaikin, Miriam.
   Esther.

   Summary: Retells the Old Testament story of how the
young Jewish girl, Esther, became Queen of Persia and used
her influence to stop the evil minister Haman from killing all
the Jews. The feast of Purim commemorates this event.
   1. Esther, Queen of Persia — Juvenile literature.
2. Iran — Kings and rulers — Biography — Juvenile literature.
3. Bible stories, English — O.T. Esther. 4. Purim —
Juvenile literature. [1. Esther, Queen of Persia.
2. Bible stories — O.T. 3. Purim] I. Rosenberry, Vera,
ill. II. Title.
BS580.E8C48   1987   222´.909505   86–20183
ISBN 0–8276–0272–3

Designed by Adrianne Onderdonk Dudden

For Jean Stein, another queen

Ahasuerus, mighty ruler of Persia and of 127 provinces, threw open the gates of his palace. He invited the people of Shushan, the capital city, to a great wine banquet. The men reclined on silver couches. They sipped wine from golden goblets. In another part of the palace the women enjoyed a banquet of their own with Vashti, the queen.

ueen Vashti is the most beautiful woman in all Persia," the king told his friends. "I will send for her. You can see for yourselves."

But Vashti refused to come. According to Persian law, a wife must obey her husband. And Vashti had disobeyed not only her husband — but the king! Ahasuerus banished Vashti from the palace, sent her away.

He was soon sorry. For he missed Vashti.

"Find a new queen," his friends said.

The king took their advice. He ordered his ministers to bring him the most beautiful young women in the land. He would look them over and choose a new queen.

Now Shushan was a large and busy city. Persians, Medes, Indians, Jews, and others lived there. One of the Jews was Mordecai, the scribe. In those days, most people could not read or write. Mordecai wrote letters and documents for them from his seat inside the palace gate.

The king's ministers arrived in the street where Mordecai lived. Esther, his orphan niece, lived with him. She was very beautiful. Mordecai told her, "If the ministers choose to bring you before the king, do not tell them that you are a Jew. There are those who would do us harm."

The ministers *did* choose Esther.

And when King Ahasuerus saw her, he fell in love with her and made her his queen.

Mordecai and Esther kept secret the fact that they were related. But each day, Mordecai stopped at the queen's gate to ask the guards how Esther was.

In the spring, in the Hebrew month of Nisan, Mordecai heard two guards plotting to poison the king. Mordecai told Esther, and Esther told the king. The king ordered the guards hanged. His secretary, who recorded all important events, recorded this event also in the royal diary.

In the same month the king promoted Haman,
a palace noble, to chief minister. Haman thought of himself as a
god to be worshiped. The people of Shushan bowed down to
Haman because of his high position. But Mordecai would not
bow to him.

Each time Mordecai refused to bow, Haman's anger grew.
One day, he decided to kill not only Mordecai, but all the
Jews. And he went to a fortuneteller to pick a lucky date
for his scheme.

The fortuneteller took up his *pur*, a stone marked "yes"
on one side and "no" on the other. "Is the first month Haman's
lucky month?" he asked, and tossed the *pur*.

The *pur* answered, "No." The fortuneteller kept tossing
the *pur* until Haman received as a lucky date the thirteenth
day of the month of Adar.

Needing the king's permission for his scheme, Haman went to the palace. "There are people in your kingdom who are different from us," he said. "They obey strange laws. They are a menace and a danger. With the king's permission, I will have them killed."

The king removed his ring. He gave it to Haman and said, "The ring is yours — the people also. Do as you see fit."

The ring was the royal seal, the king's own signature. With it Haman could pass laws. He passed this law and sent copies throughout the kingdom:

To all governors in Persia and in the 127 provinces. Attention! Kill all Jews, young and old, on the thirteenth of Adar, and seize their possessions.

A copy of the law was posted in Shushan. And when Mordecai and the Jews read it, they wept and cried aloud.

Esther, in the palace, heard their cries. She sent a servant to find out what had happened. Mordecai gave the servant a copy of the law for Esther. He also sent her this message: "Go to the king. Speak to him. Save your people."

To this Esther answered, "I am not allowed to go before the king unless he sends for me."

"You must," replied Mordecai. "Don't think you will escape harm on the thirteenth of Adar. Besides, it is possible that you became queen so that you could save your people."

Esther agreed. She asked Mordecai and all the Jews to pray for her safety and to fast for three days. She planned to do the same. "Then I will go in to the king," she said. "And if I perish, I perish."

After the fast, Esther put on a royal gown and went to see the king. She was frightened. The king had not sent for her. He might order the guards to seize her, or have her beheaded for coming without permission. Instead, he received her kindly. He raised his scepter to her and invited her in.

"What is your wish, my queen?" Ahasuerus asked. "I am prepared to give you up to half my kingdom."

"If it please the king," Esther said, "let him come with his chief minister to a wine banquet that I have prepared."

The king sent his servants to fetch Haman. And he and the chief minister went in to Esther's banquet.

"What is your wish, my queen?" the king asked again as Esther's servant poured wine. "I am prepared to give you up to half my kingdom."

Esther still did not tell Ahasuerus the real reason for her banquet. "Let the king and his chief minister come here again tomorrow," she said. "I will speak of it then."

Haman left the palace feeling mighty. What an honor he had received. He had been the only guest of the king and queen! Everyone moved aside to make way for him — everyone but Mordecai, who remained standing where he was.

Haman spoke of his fury to his wife and ten sons. "The queen honored me today," he said. "She will honor me again tomorrow. But it all means nothing to me when I see the Jew, Mordecai. Why must I wait to see him dead?"

"Why wait?" asked his wife. "Order a gallows made, and in the morning go to the king and ask for permission to hang Mordecai."

Haman did as his wife suggested — he ordered a gallows.

Meanwhile, in the palace the king could not sleep. To pass the time, his secretary read aloud to him from the royal diary. The secretary read how Mordecai had saved the king's life. "What honor did I bestow upon Mordecai?" the king asked.

"None," said the secretary.

Outside, Haman arrived in the courtyard to ask the king for permission to hang Mordecai.

"Haman wishes to see the king," the guard announced.

"Let him enter," the king said.

"There is a man I wish to honor," the king told Haman. "What shall I do for him?"

Haman was sure the honor was for himself. "Let the man be seen riding the king's horse, on whose head a royal crown has been set," he said. "And let a palace noble lead him through the streets crying, 'Here is the man the king wishes to honor!'"

"Do as you suggest," said the king. "You are the palace noble. Mordecai is the man I wish to honor."

Bitter and ashamed, Haman led Mordecai through the streets crying, "Here is the man the king wishes to honor!"

Later, when Haman sat reclining beside the king at Esther's banquet, he tried to hide his feelings behind a smile.

"You promised to speak of your wish today, my queen," Ahasuerus said to Esther.

Now, at last, Esther told the king what was in her heart. "A law has been passed in your name saying that my people and I are to be killed."

The king leaped from his couch. "Who would dare do such a thing?" he asked.

"This evil man," Esther said as she pointed to Haman.

Harbonah, a guard, said, "What's more, your Majesty, Haman has built a gallows. He plans to hang Mordecai this very night."

"Hang Haman on it instead!" the king cried.

Esther now told the king that Mordecai was her uncle. And when Mordecai came before the king, the king gave Mordecai the ring he had taken from Haman. And he named Mordecai the new chief minister.

All would have been well but for Haman's law. Esther threw herself at the king's feet. "Please cancel Haman's evil decree. Let my people live," she pleaded.

The king lifted her up. "Not even the king can cancel a royal decree in the Persian empire," he said. "But Mordecai now wears my ring. He can pass whatever law he wishes concerning the Jews."

This was the law that Mordecai passed and sent throughout the kingdom:

To all governors in Persia and in the 127 provinces. Attention! Let the Jews organize to defend themselves on the thirteenth of Adar. Let them slay their attackers.

Mordecai was now a great man in Persia. How proud the Jews were to see him in his robes of royal blue and wearing a crown upon his head. Nevertheless, on the thirteenth of Adar the evildoers rose up to slay the Jews. But the opposite happened. The Jews slew their attackers instead, including the ten sons of Haman.

Upon Esther's request, the king ordered Haman's ten sons hung in the public square as a warning to any who would harm the Jews.

The Jews celebrated their rescue with great rejoicing and a feast. And Esther and Mordecai wrote a letter to all Jews throughout the kingdom telling them to celebrate the rescue forever. They called the holiday Purim because of the *pur*.

From that day more than two thousand years ago, Jews all over the world celebrate Purim each year on the fourteenth and fifteenth of Adar. They read aloud Esther's story, send presents to one another, and make merry.